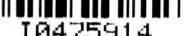
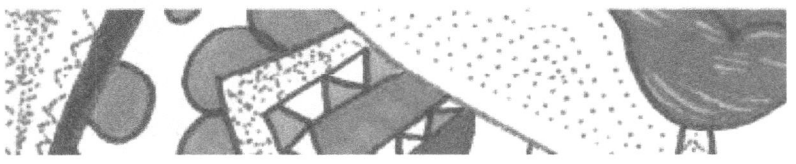

Abstract Faces
Carry Along

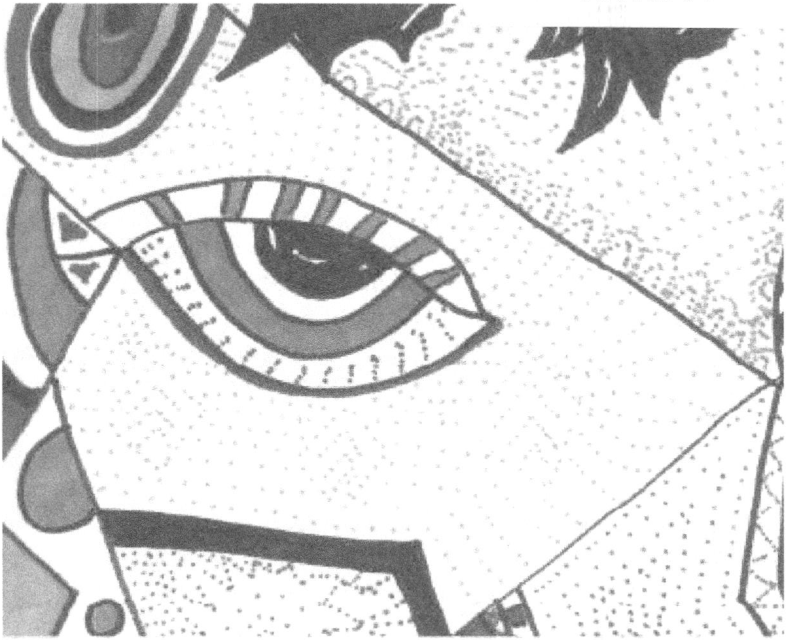

Melissa Caudle

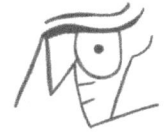

OPEN DOOR PUBLISHING COMPANY

NEW ORLEANS, LOUISIANA

Abstract Faces Carry Along Vol I is an abstract art collection by artist Melissa Caudle. Embrace the uniqueness of each face and the inner beauty they behold as you bring life with your touch. Each drawing is limitless in opportunity. Use your imagination as you create your own tangles, zendangles, dots, flowers etc. I love to create patterns with dots to vary larger white spaces. That is one of my own signature pattern in my original art. Make each drawing your own creation. Simply relax and enjoy yourself. You have complete freedom to express yourself. There is only one rule for a colorist – there are no rules. The artist strongly advises to put a piece of cardstock or file folder behind each page as you color to avoid bleed through. Each drawing is printed on one side making them suitable for framing by cutting them from the book.

Bibliographical Note

Abstract Faces Vol I Coloring Book is a new work created by artist, Melissa Caudle. Her art is for sell on E-bay. To obtain original pieces of her, contact the artist at: melabstractart@gmail.com. She is also available for commissioned pieces.

www.drmelissacaudle.com   melabstractart@gmail.com

INTERNATIONAL STANDARD BOOK NUMBER

ISBN-13: 978-1542801409   ISBN-10: 1542801400

Manufactured in the United States by CreateSpace 2017

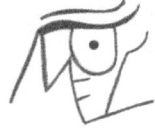

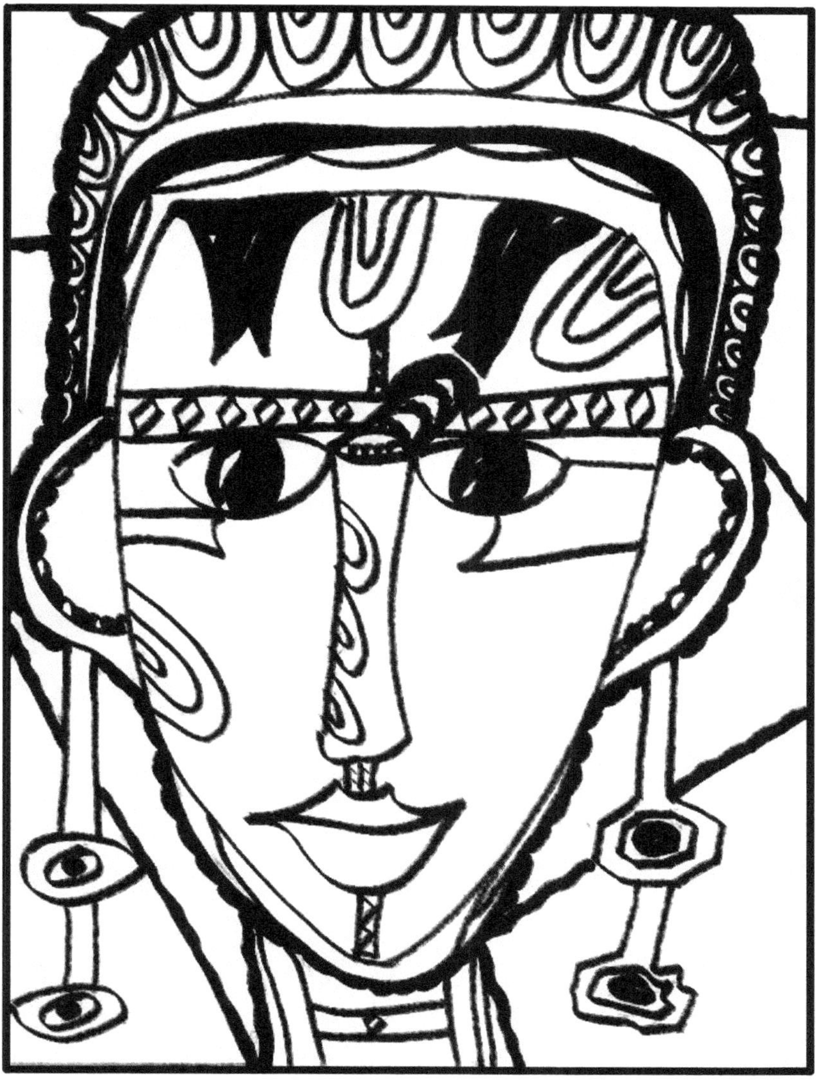

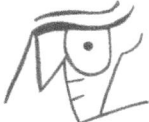

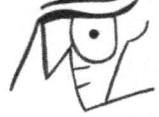

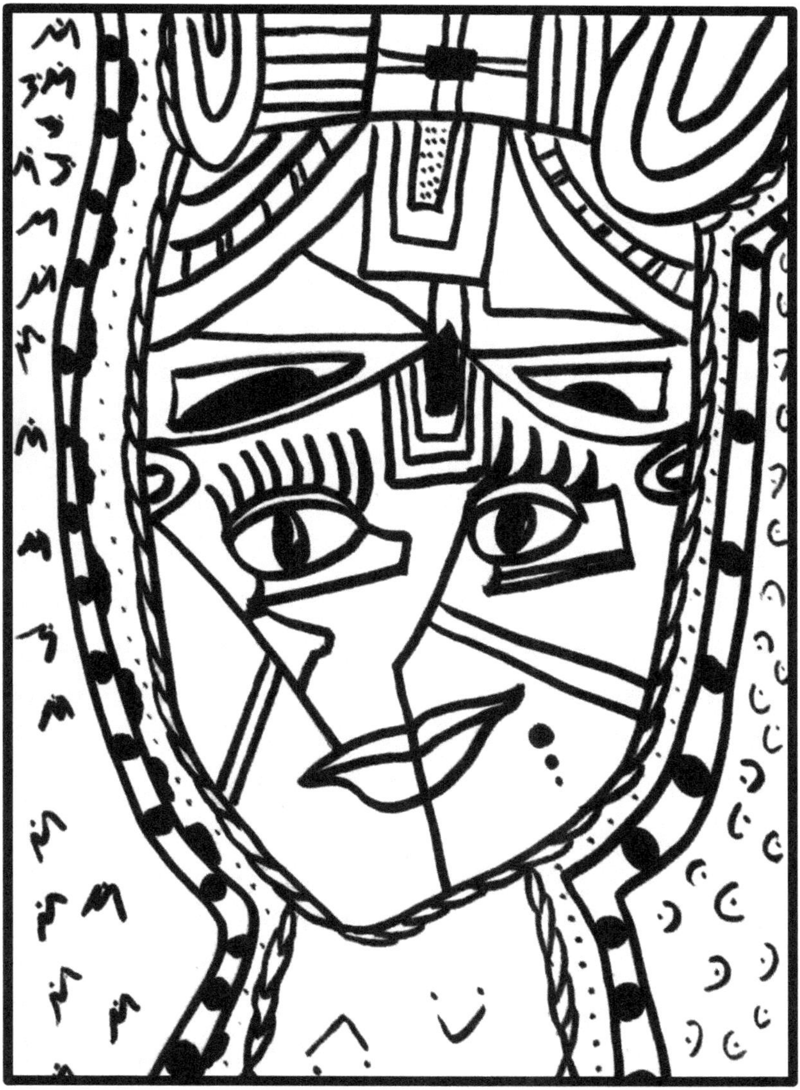

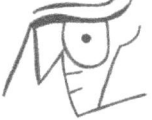

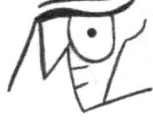

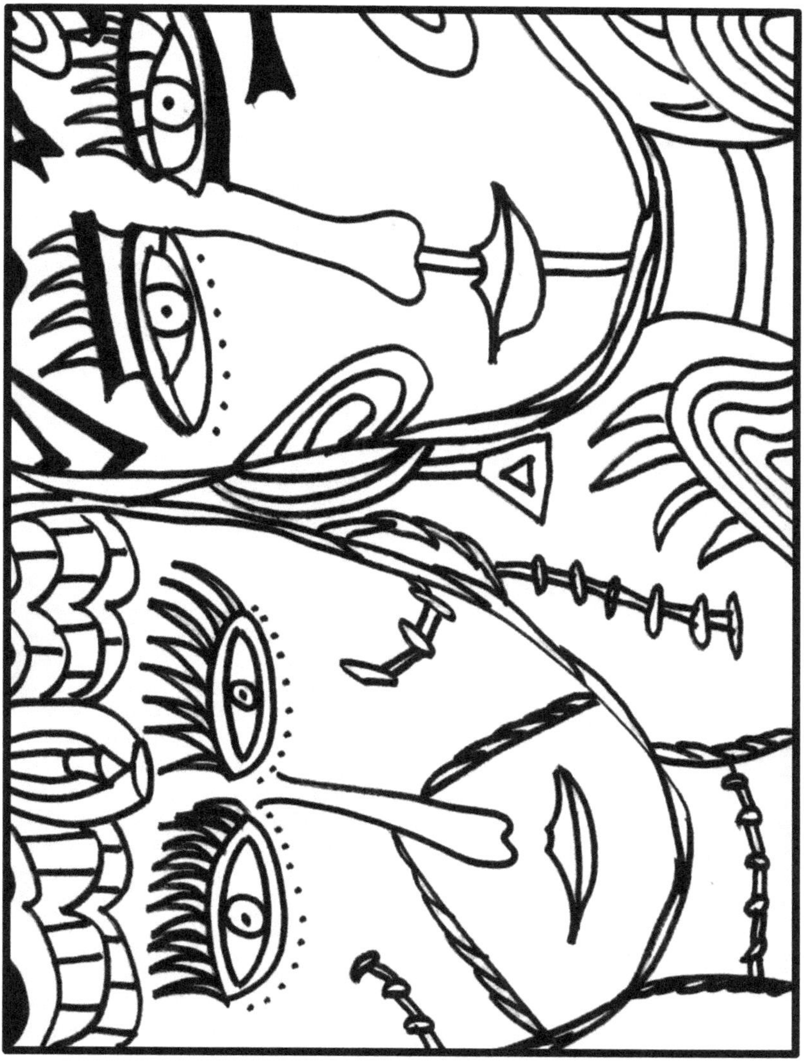

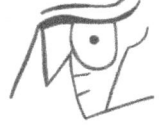

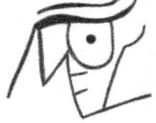

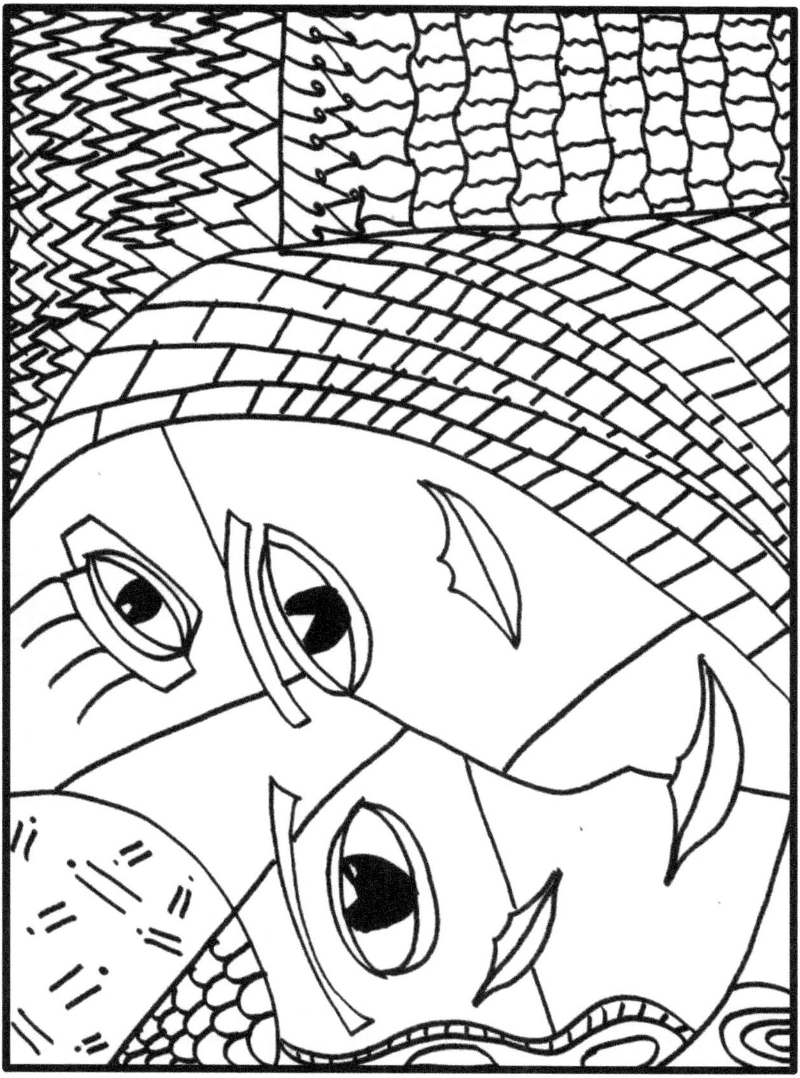

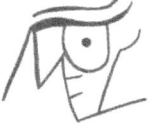

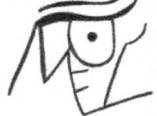

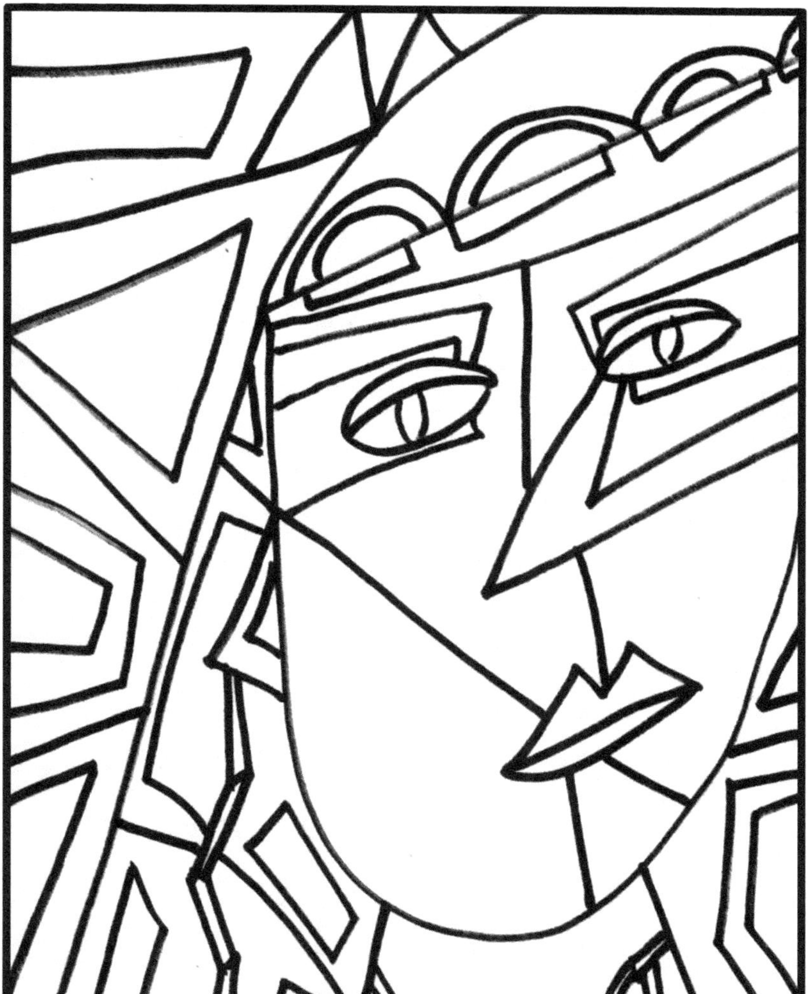

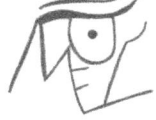

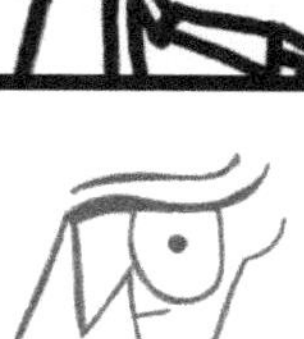

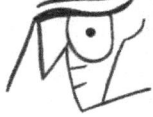

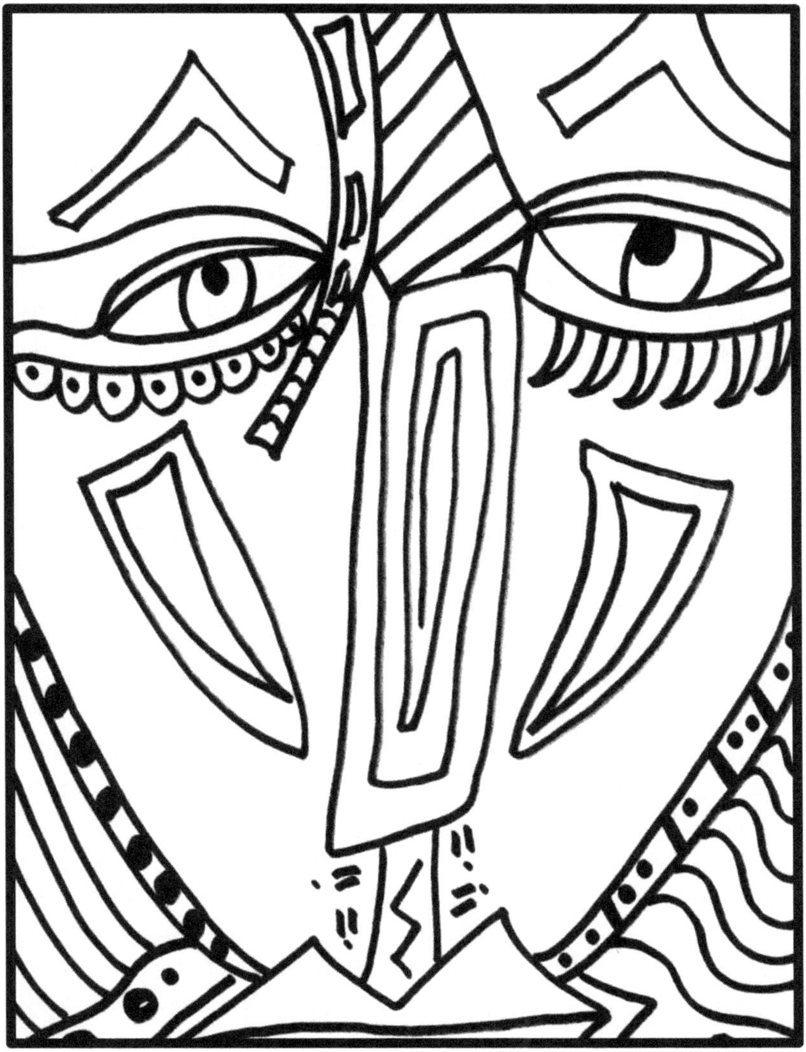

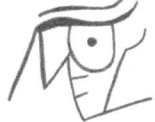

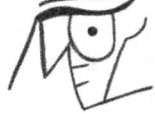

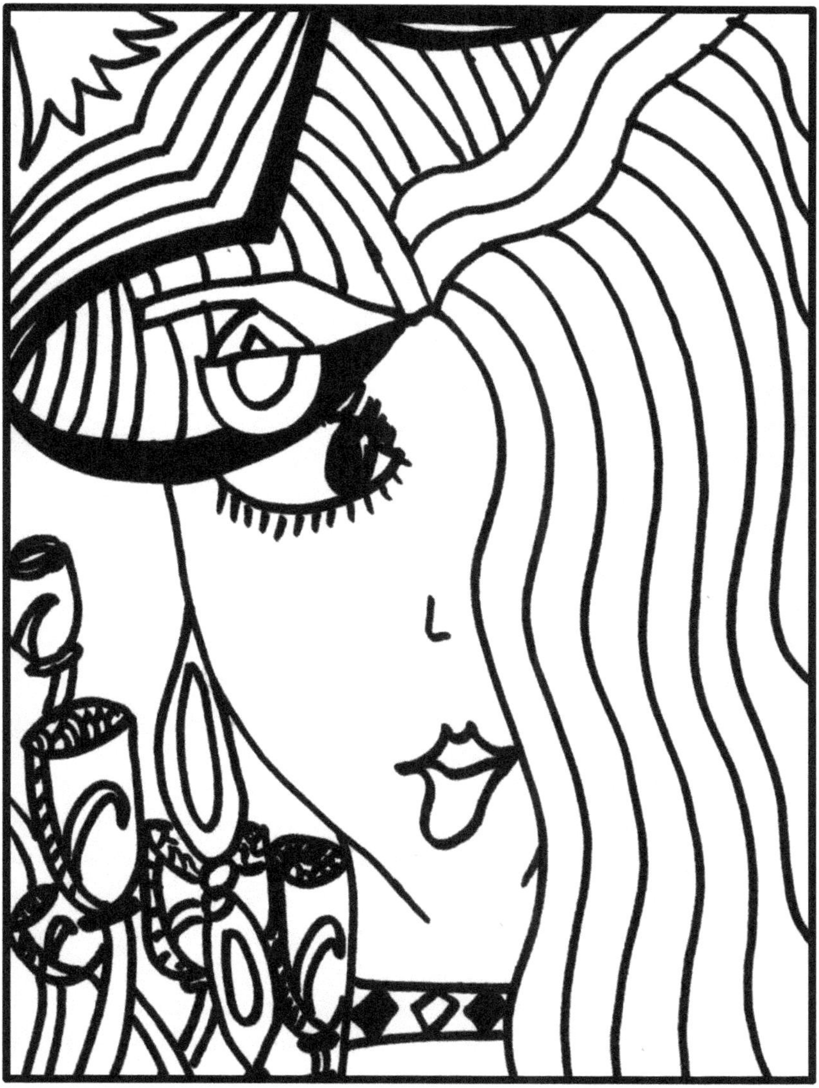

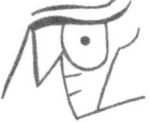

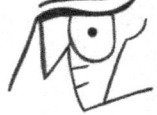

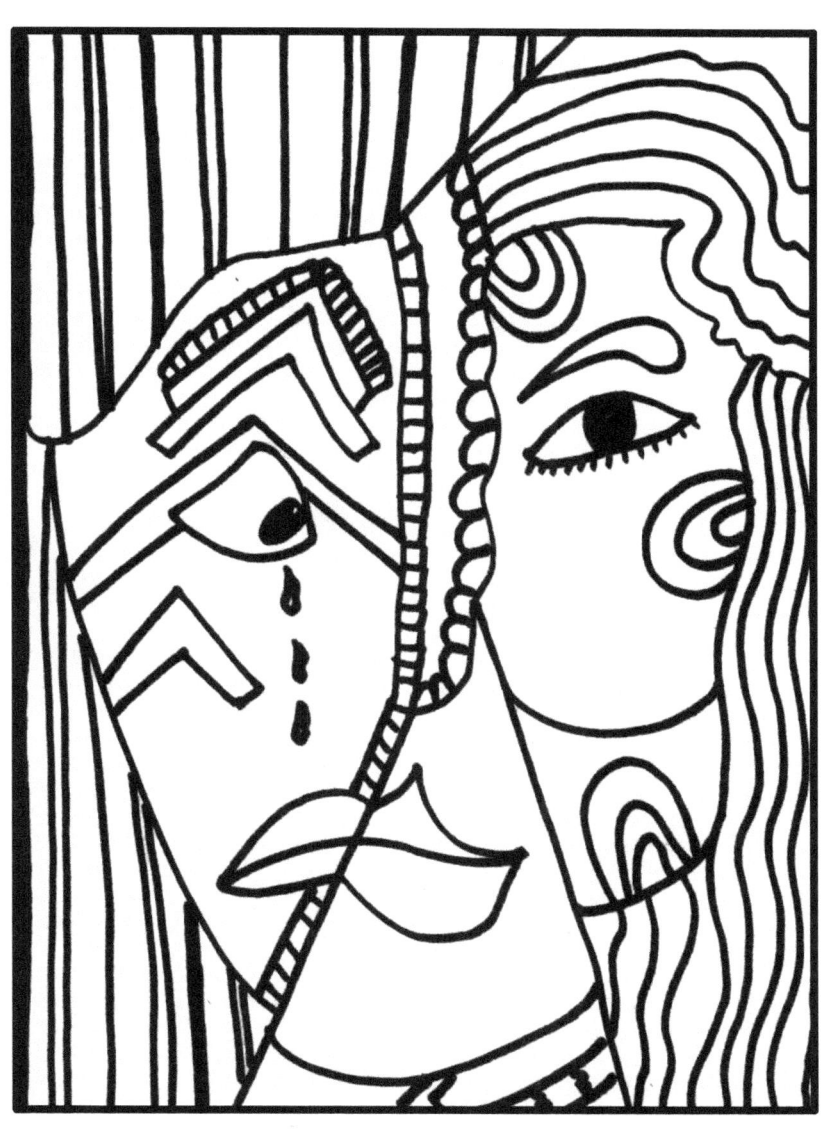

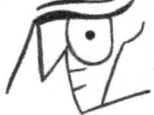

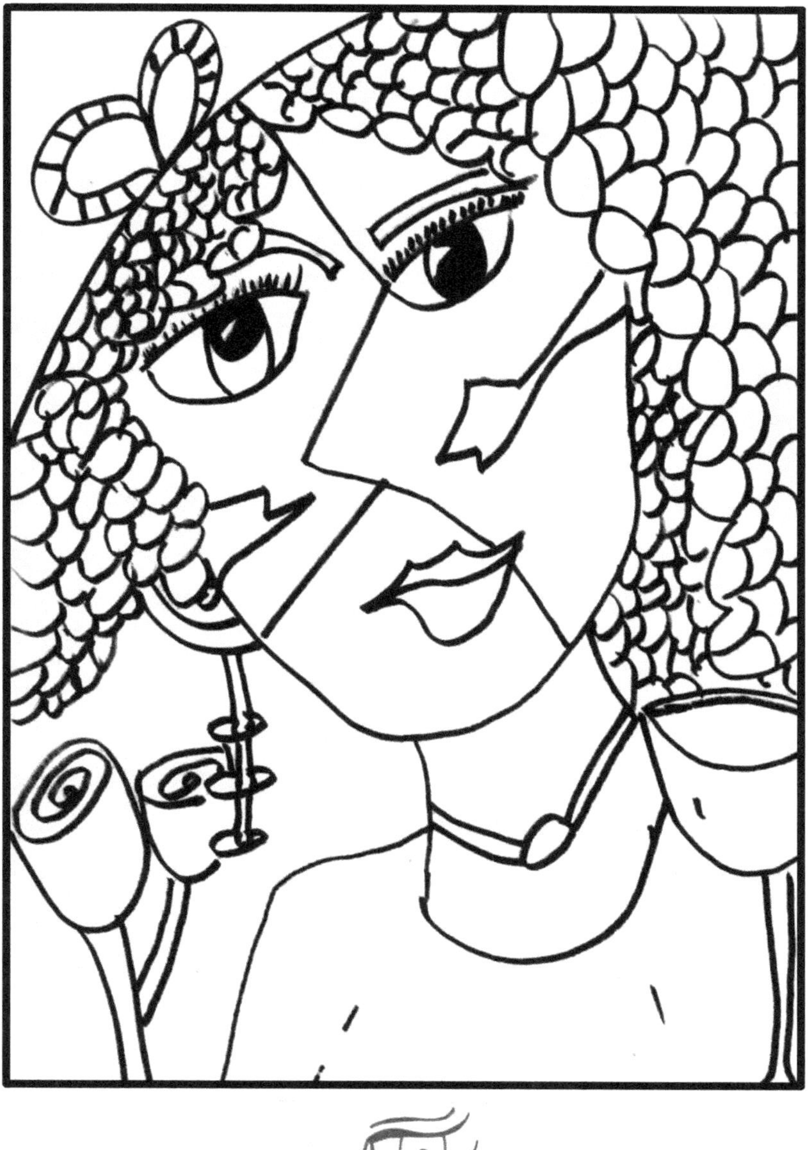

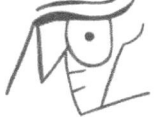

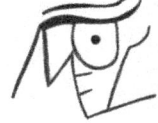

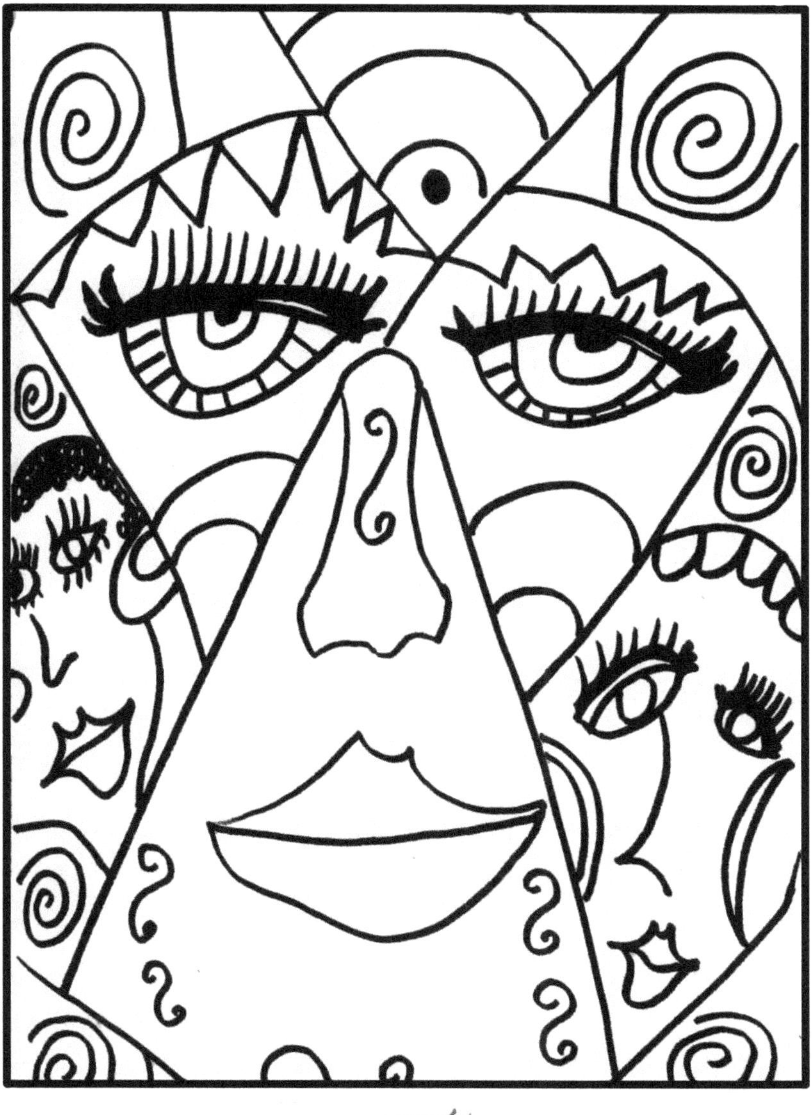

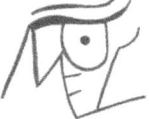

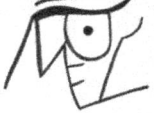

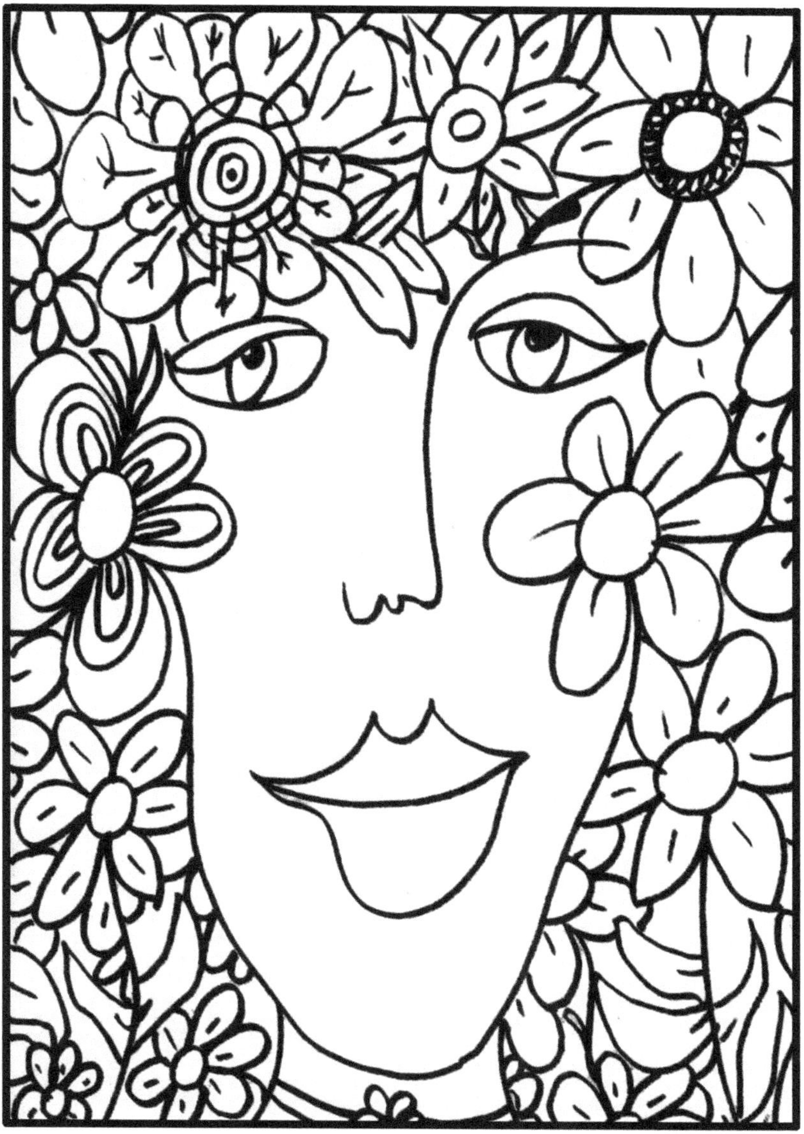

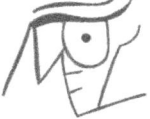

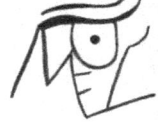

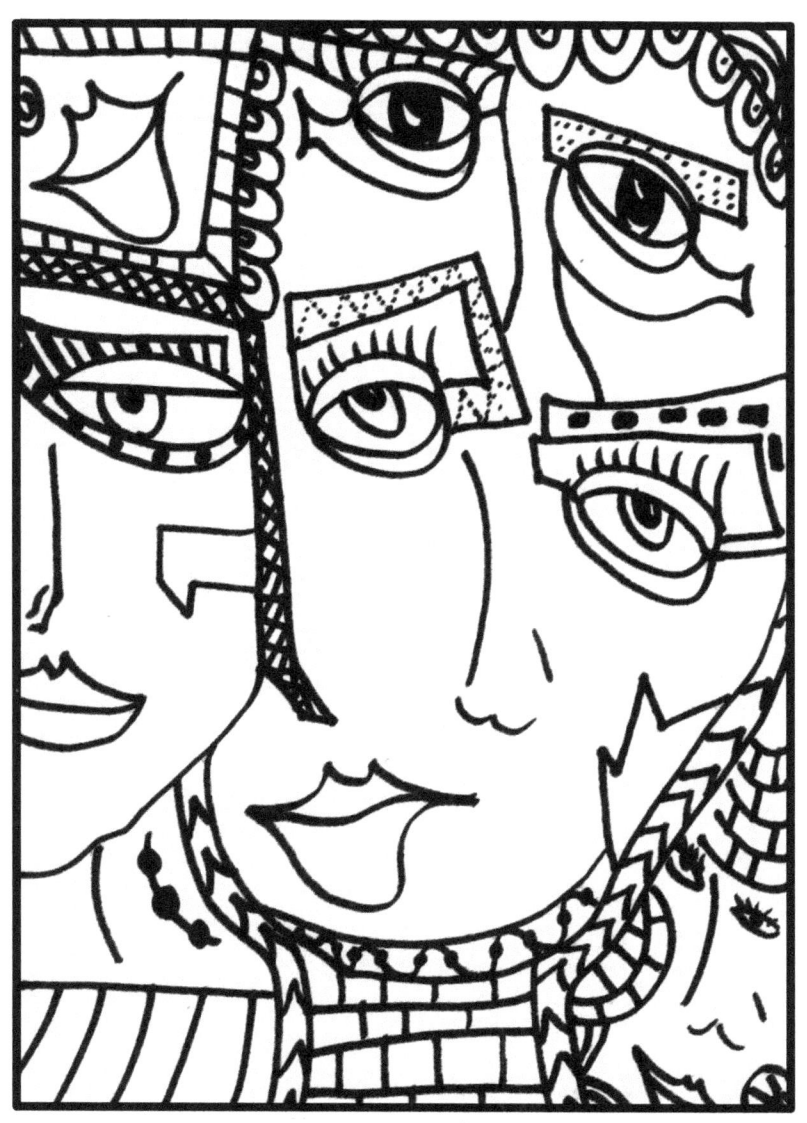

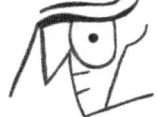

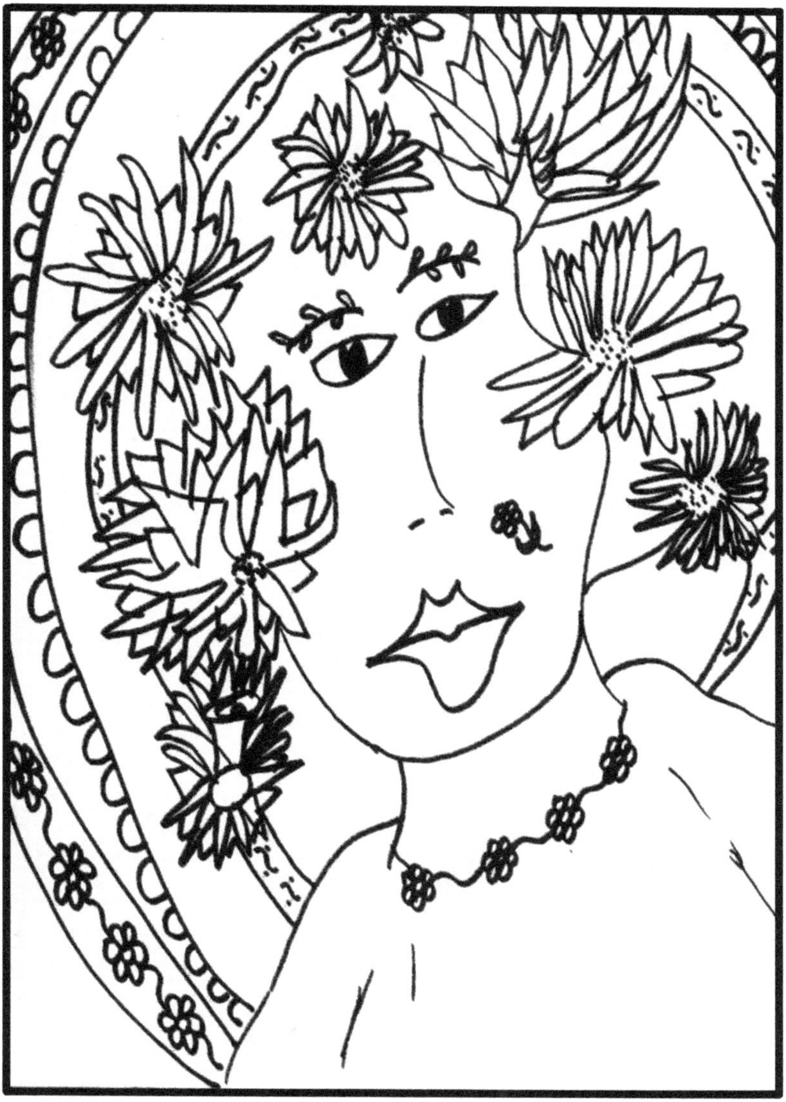

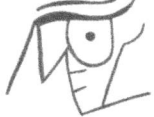

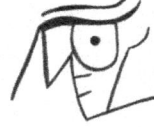

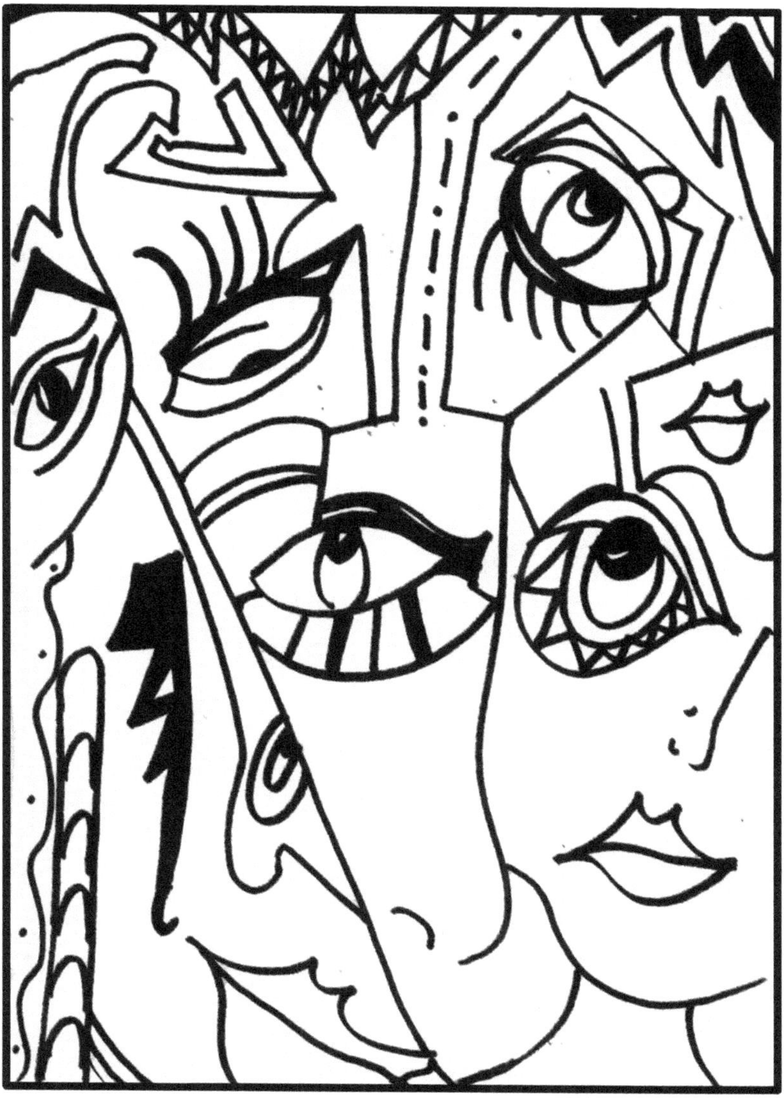

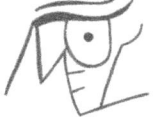

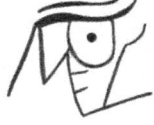

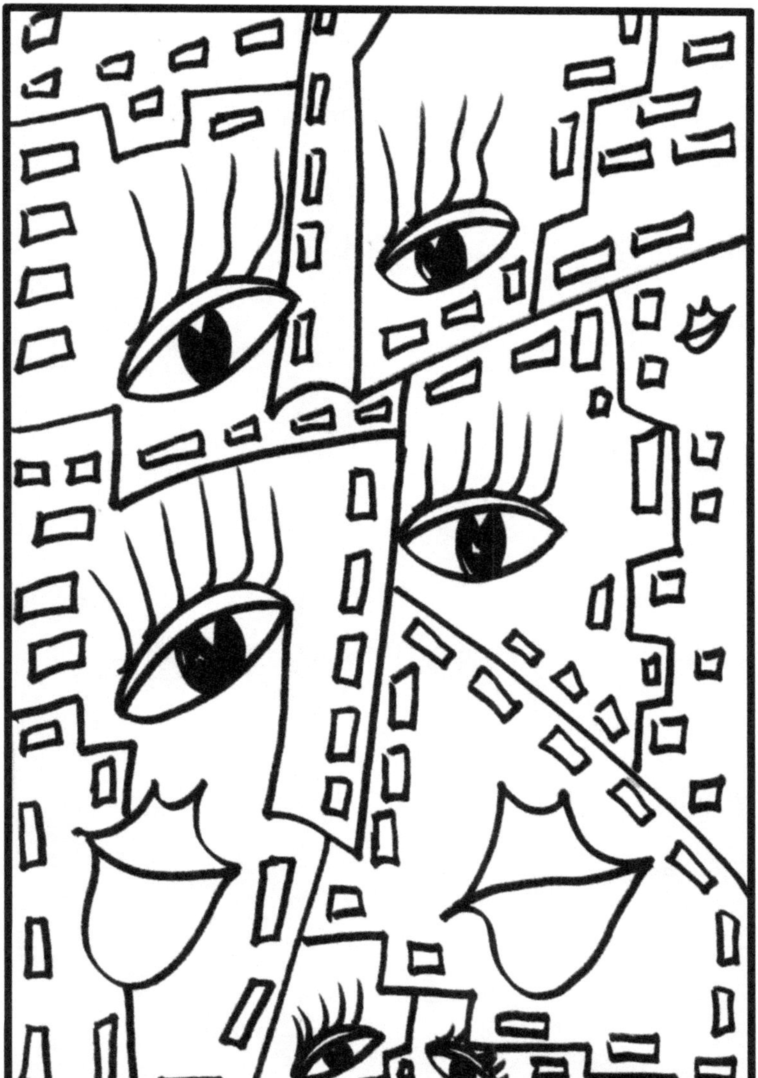

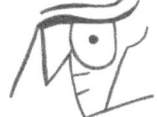

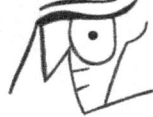

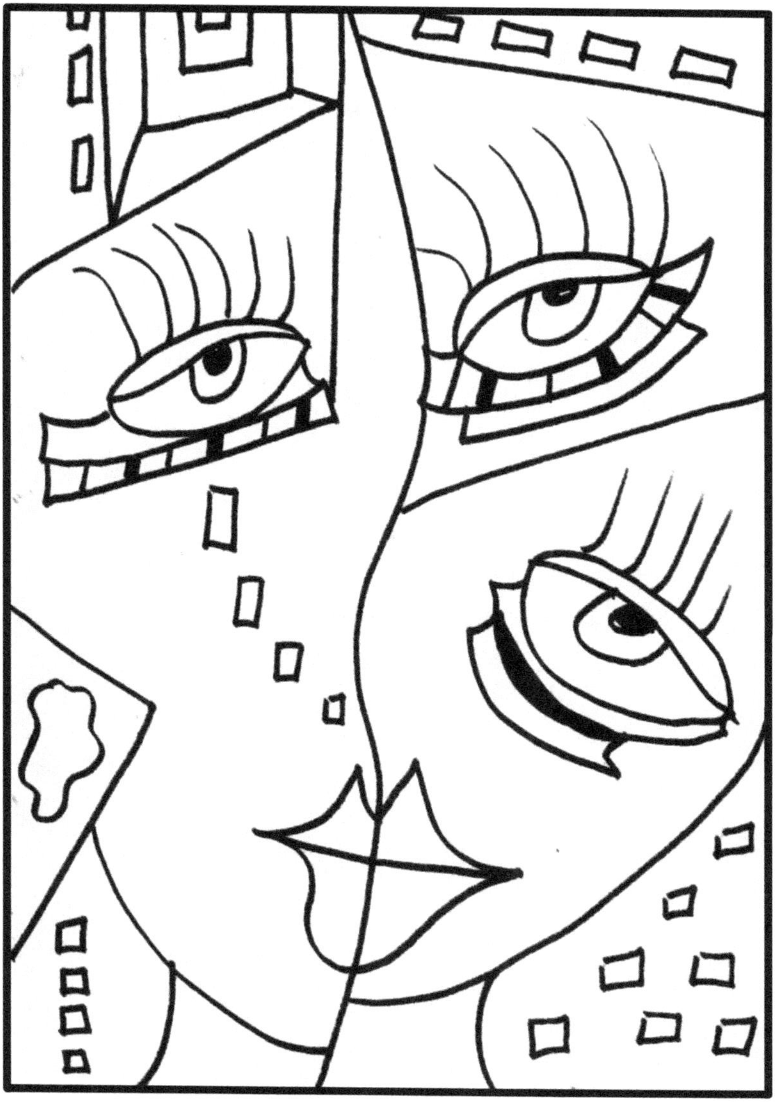

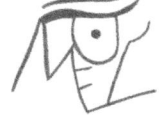

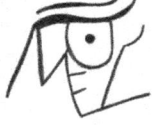

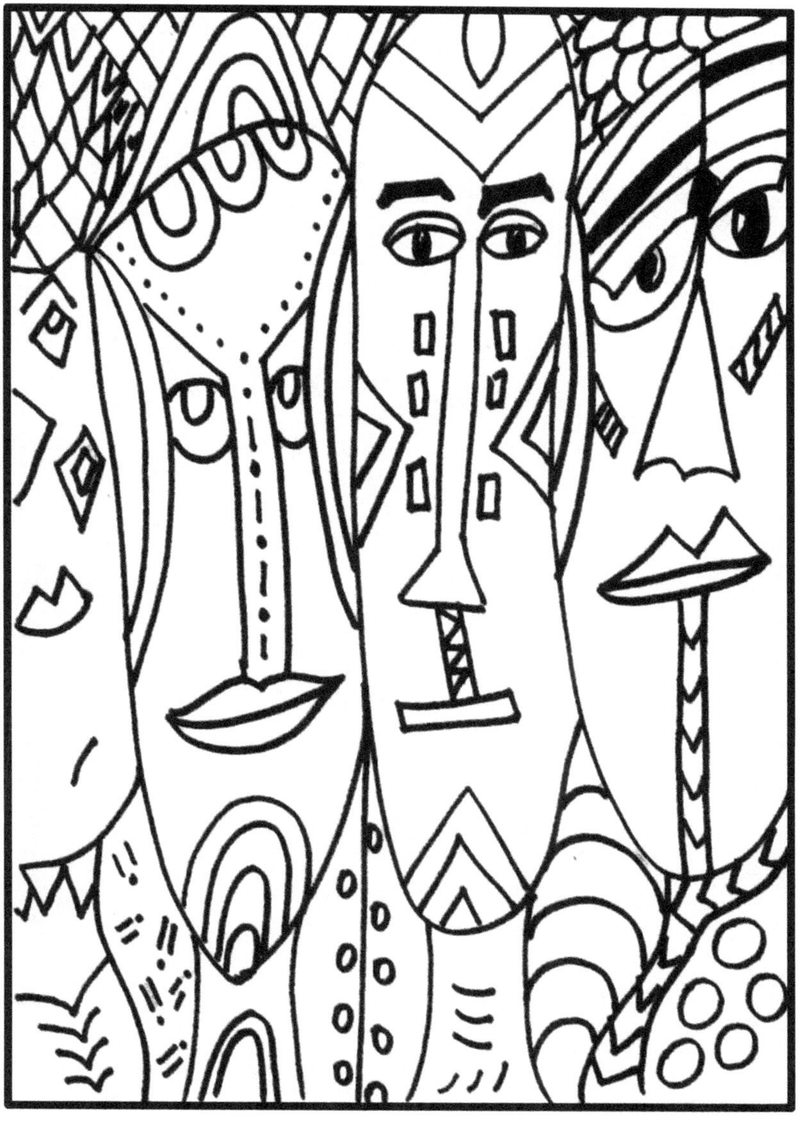

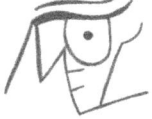

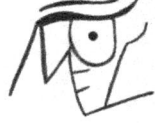

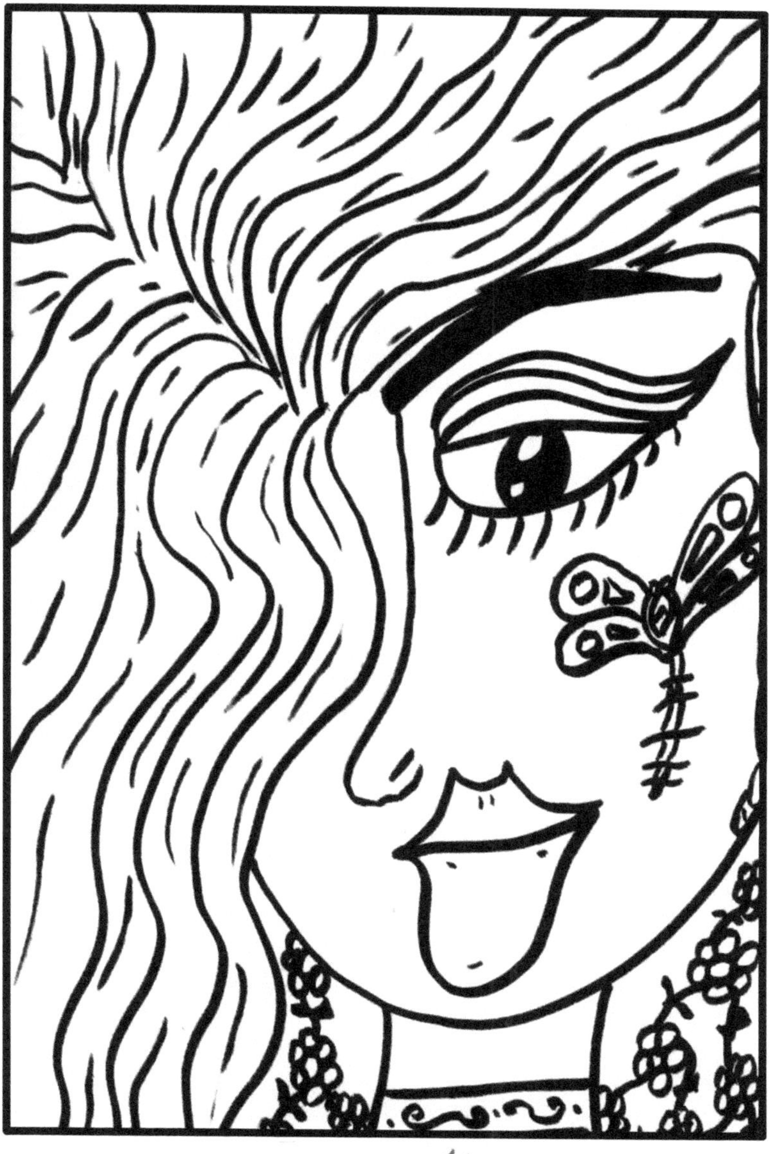

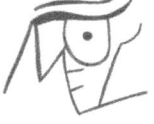

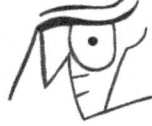

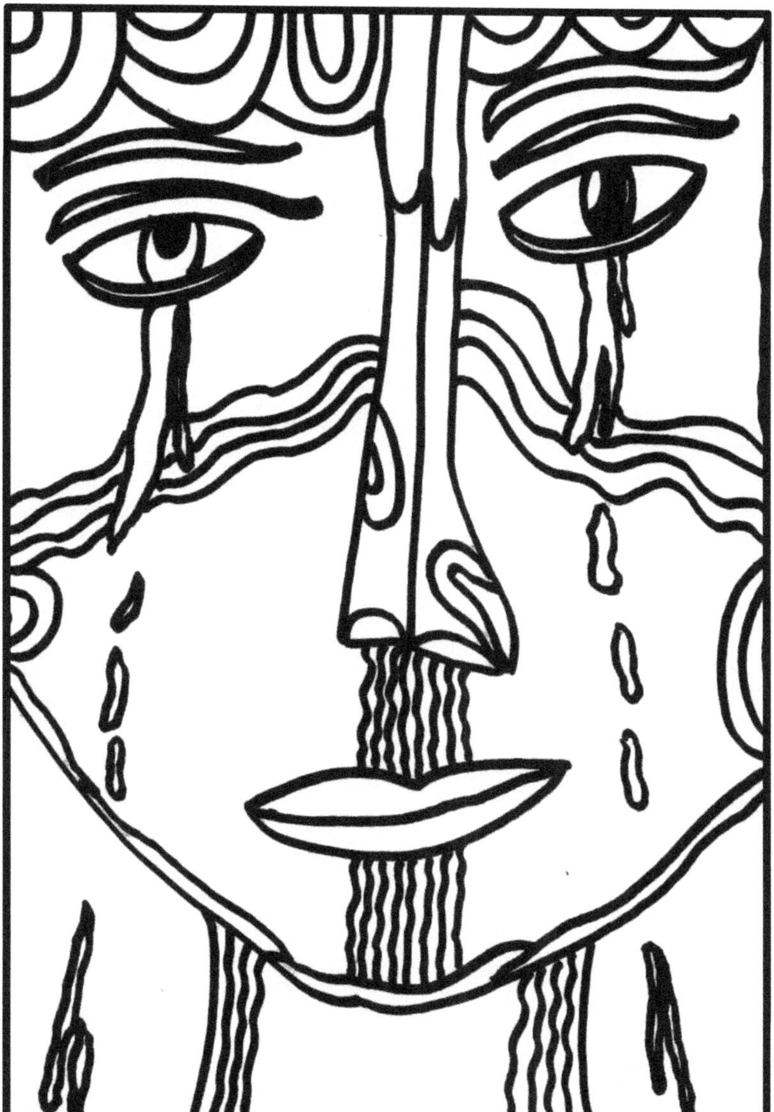

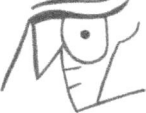

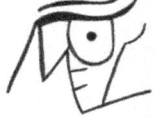

ADULT COLORING BOOKS BY MELISSA CAUDLE

www.drmelissacaudle.com

Abstract Faces Vol I

Abstract Faces Carry Along Vol I

Abstract Faces Vol II

Abstract Faces Vol III

Alien Faces Vol I

Mardi Gras Floats Vol I

ORIGINAL ART BY MELISSA CAUDLE

Melissa Caudle sells her original art from her website: www.drmelissacaudle.com and on E-bay. Several of the original drawings included in this book, colored by the artist, may still be available for sale. They are a collector's item. All art is accompanied by a Certificate of Authenticity and signed by the artist.

Email: melabstractart@gmail.com

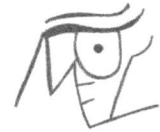

www.ingramcontent.com/pod-product-compliance
Lightning Source LLC
Chambersburg PA
CBHW070719180526
45167CB00004B/1544